A KEY TO HAPPINESS

FORGIVENESS

31 DAYS DEVOTIONAL ON FORGIVENESS

By
DR OKWUDILI JAMES EZEH

Forgiveness

*A Key to Happiness
31 Days Devotional on
Forgiveness*

by
Dr Okwudili James Ezeh

Copyright © 2016 Dr Okwudili James Ezeh

Published in United Kingdom
by Agape Behaviour Publishing
all rights reserved.

This book is protected under the copyright laws. This book may not be copied or reprinted for commercial gain or profit. The use of short quotations or occasional page copying for personal or group study is permitted and encouraged. Permission will be granted upon request.

For more information contact

Telephone: +44 (0) 8432 894 017
Mobile: +44 (0) 7939 996 111
www.agapebehaviourpublishing.com
info@agapebehaviourpublishing.com

Print ISBN: 978-1-78650-010-6
EBook ISBN: 978-1-78650-011-3

All Scripture quotations, unless otherwise indicated, taken from the New King James Version®
Copyright © 1982 by Thomas Nelson used by permission.
All rights reserved.

CONTENTS

Day 1 3
Day 2 4
Day 3 5
Day 4 6
Day 5 7
Day 6 8
Day 7 9
Day 8 10
Day 9 11
Day 10 12
Day 11 13
DAY 12 14
Day 13 15
Day 14 16
Day 15 17
Day 16 18
Day 17 19
Day 18 20
Day 19 21

Day 20 22
Day 21 23
Day 22 24
Day 23 25
Day 24 26
Day 25 27
Day 26 28
Day 27 29
Day 28 30
Day 29 31
Day 30 32
Day 31 33
Further Reading & Meditation 34
Notes 102

*This book is dedicated to my God Almighty,
my beautiful and supportive wife Nkem Katarzyna Ezeh,
my amazing children Prince Okwudili Emmanuel Ezeh
and Okwudili Judah Ezeh, my siblings,
parents and special church family in Poland,
Imago Dei Ministries and last but not least
the special person reading this book.*

*This book is a practical guide on forgiveness.
I am confident that as you read this book
you will develop the faith, joy, power and sensitivity to
forgive and understand the importance of continuous
forgiveness.*

This book is to help you to do the following

- ✓ 31 days to free your pain through FORGIVENESS
- ✓ Release your pain through FORGIVENESS
- ✓ Live a lifestyle of FORGIVENESS and HAPPINESS
- ✓ Totally FORGIVE in 31 days and release your pain

Day 1

Matthew 6:12. Romans 5:6-11 (Please Read)
Forgiveness, just like love is a DECISION not a FEELING.

¹² And forgive us our debts, as we forgive our debtors.

Expectation is the foundation or bases for miracle. Lack of expectation is like driving without a destination.

Choose to expect new and great things in your life for that is the WILL OF GOD IN CHRIST OVER YOU. He gives strength to the Weak

Isaiah 40:29-31 (Please Read)

Your God shall meet with you in Jesus name.

_____
_____
_____
_____
_____

Day 2

Matthew 6:12. Romans 5:6-11 *(Please Read)*
Forgiveness, just like love is a DECISION not a FEELING.
[12] And forgive us our debts, as we forgive our debtors.

Sounds control our environment including our feelings.
That's why people jump like crazy in clubs even when they don't understand the music.

Allow sounds of PRAISE AND WORSHIP to fill your heart and your environment today to heal you and your family in Jesus name.

Psalms 150:6 *(Please Read)*
Your day of joy and singing is here.

_____

_____

_____

_____

_____

Day 3

Matthew 6:12. Romans 5:6-11 *(Please Read)*
Forgiveness, just like love is a DECISION not a FEELING.

¹² And forgive us our debts, as we forgive our debtors.

Choose Godly and bold friends that will look you in the face and tell you the truth. Don't hang around friends that only nurse their pains but don't know how to forgive and let go because over time, you will become like your friends.

1 Corinthians 15:33 *(Please Read)*

May God bless you with genuine relationships in Jesus name.

_____

_____

_____

_____

_____

Day 4

Matthew 6:12. Romans 5:6-11 *(Please Read)*
Forgiveness, just like love is a DECISION not a FEELING.

12 And forgive us our debts, as we forgive our debtors.

As difficult as it may appear to be, it's better to be the one receiving the pain than the one giving the pain.

Why? It denotes who is stronger in a relationship after all children are the ones always making a mess. Secondly consequences of inflicting pain are bigger than the pain inflicted.

May your heart be healed in Jesus name.

_____

_____

_____

_____

_____

Day 5

Matthew 6:12. Romans 5:6-11 *(Please Read)*
Forgiveness, just like love is a DECISION not a FEELING.
[12] And forgive us our debts, as we forgive our debtors.

I believe that the reason why you have your eyes in front is that God wants you to always look forward. Secondly there is nothing that happened to you that the future can't recover for you.

Your better days are in front of you.

Isaiah 43:19 (Please Read).

Your better days are fast coming in Jesus name.

_____
_____
_____
_____
_____

Day 6

Matthew 6:12. Romans 5:6-11 *(Please Read)*
Forgiveness, just like love is a DECISION not a FEELING.
¹² And forgive us our debts, as we forgive our debtors.

One of the ways of getting healed from hurt and pain is to PRAY FOR those that hurt you. Remember not PRAYING ABOUT THEM BUT PRAYING FOR THEM.

Luke 6:27-29, Romans 12:14 *(Please Read).*

Your healing and recovery is in FORGIVENESS therefore, I pray that You will receive strength to forgive in Jesus name.

_____

_____

_____

_____

_____

Day 7

Matthew 6:12. Romans 5:6-11 *(Please Read)*
Forgiveness, just like love is a DECISION not a FEELING.
¹² And forgive us our debts, as we forgive our debtors.

If you are going to shift the responsibility of your healing from your offender to yourself, you must learn how to release your pain to GOD, who is the ONLY ONE who understands ALL about pain and injustice.
This you do in faith through PRAYER.

1Peter 5:7 *(Please Read)*

This time you are going to receive true healing in Jesus name.

_____
_____
_____
_____
_____

Day 8

Matthew 6:12. Romans 5:6-11 *(Please Read)*
Forgiveness, just like love is a DECISION not a FEELING.

¹² And forgive us our debts, as we forgive our debtors.

Yesterday is dead and tomorrow may never come. Your life is NOW, therefore do not let the pain and experience of yesterday to steal, kill or destroy the beauty of today.

Today is God's gift to you, please, enjoy it in PRAISE.

Psalms 118:24 *(Please Read).*
I PRAY FOR YOU THAT YOUR LIFE WILL NOT BE BUILT ON BITTERNESS in Jesus name.

_____

_____

_____

_____

_____

Day 9

Matthew 6:12. Romans 5:6-11 (Please Read)
Forgiveness, just like love is a DECISION not a FEELING.

¹² And forgive us our debts, as we forgive our debtors.

Any success, friendship, marriage, church that is built on bitterness, REVENGE or showoff, must be maintained through pain and will NEVER LAST.

You have to let go if you don't want to have EMPTINESS at the centre of your 'SUCCESS'.

I PRAY FOR YOU THAT YOUR LIFE WILL NOT BE BUILT ON BITTERNESS in Jesus name.

_____

_____

_____

_____

_____

Day 10

Matthew 6:12. Romans 5:6-11 (Please Read)
Forgiveness, just like love is a DECISION not a FEELING.
¹² And forgive us our debts, as we forgive our debtors.

Whoever that CAN'T or WOULDN'T help you become your best, also CAN'T or WON'T stop you from becoming your best.

God is still GOING to do a NEW THING in you with or without the person that hurt you because you are His.

Isaiah 43:19 (Please Read)
I declare this day that you shall become THE best that God made you to be in Jesus name.

_____

_____

_____

_____

_____

Day 11

Matthew 6:12. Romans 5:6-11 *(Please Read)*
Forgiveness, just like love is a DECISION not a FEELING.
¹² And forgive us our debts, as we forgive our debtors.

Never Place the burden or the expectation of your healing and restoration on the one who hurt you or on a human being. Firstly, they don't have such power. Secondly, HEALING IS GOD'S GIFT AND GOD'S ALONE.

Psalms 147:13 *(Please Read).*

Try Him, He is always available and waiting.
May all your hurt and pain be cleansed in Jesus name.

_____
_____
_____
_____
_____

DAY 12

Matthew 6:12. Romans 5:6-11 (Please Read)
Forgiveness, just like love is a DECISION not a FEELING.
¹² And forgive us our debts, as we forgive our debtors.

Genesis 50:17 (NKJV)
¹⁷ 'Thus you shall say to Joseph: "I beg you, please forgive the trespass of your brothers and their sin; for they did evil to you."

Now, please, forgive the trespass of the servants of the God of your father." And Joseph wept when they spoke to him.

People may do bad things to you, but nevertheless PLEASE forgive.

_____
_____
_____
_____
_____

Day 13

Matthew 6:12. Romans 5:6-11 *(Please Read)*
Forgiveness, just like love is a DECISION not a FEELING.
¹² And forgive us our debts, as we forgive our debtors.

You can't OUTLIVE, OUTGIVE or OUTTHINK THE ONE WHO MADE TIME, AND PLACED YOU IN TIME AND MADE YOUR MIND.
Just like Lazarus sister, you're asking God for a MINI miracle while Jesus desires to give you a MEGA miracle.

John 11:32-44 *(Please Read)*

Maintain a forgiving heart and get ready for MEGA MIRACLES from the greatest giver in Jesus name.

_____

_____

_____

_____

_____

Day 14

Matthew 6:12. Romans 5:6-11 *(Please Read)*
Forgiveness, just like love is a DECISION not a FEELING.

¹² And forgive us our debts, as we forgive our debtors.

Forgive and forget, is it possible?

YES IT IS. Just let God be TRUE, as a citizen of heaven God has a way of blessing and lifting you so high so much so that what used to hurt you won't hurt you anymore.

Hebrews 6:14 *(Please Read)*

Get ready to be graced and blessed out of your troubles, pain and hurt in Jesus name.

_____

_____

_____

_____

_____

Day 15

Matthew 6:12. Romans 5:6-11 *(Please Read)*
Forgiveness, just like love is a DECISION not a FEELING.
¹² And forgive us our debts, as we forgive our debtors.

Time, they say is a great healer.
IT'S THE PRODUCT OF TIME (what happens within the time) THAT HEALS AND NOT JUST TIME ITSELF. Finding solace in recounting and complaining about your pain will never make the pain go away.
So be wiser, give your pain to Jesus.

Psalm 34:18 *(Please Read)*
May your life become a living testimony in Jesus name.

_____

_____

_____

_____

Day 16

Matthew 6:12. Romans 5:6-11 *(Please Read)*
Forgiveness, just like love is a DECISION not a FEELING.
¹² And forgive us our debts, as we forgive our debtors.
Forgiveness enlarges your sphere and scope of trust, love, experience and existence.
The larger your sphere of operations, the more qualified you are to sympathize and empathize with people.
As a result this makes you a better and more experienced person.
2 Corinthians 4:17 *(Please Read)*
May your life become a walking wisdom in Jesus name.

_____

_____

_____

_____

_____

Day 17

Matthew 6:12. Romans 5:6-11 (Please Read)
Forgiveness, just like love is a DECISION not a FEELING.

¹² And forgive us our debts, as we forgive our debtors.

Your life might be under a negative gene control also known as GENERATIONAL CURSE.
Your grandparents got divorced, your parents divorced and now you are tempted to do the same all because of the curse of UNFORGIVENESS.
UNFORGIVENESS is a negative demonic chain that has to be destroyed.
1 Peter 2:9 (Please Read)
Your chains are destroyed by the BLOOD of JESUS in Jesus name.

_____

_____

_____

_____

_____

Day 18

Matthew 6:12. Romans 5:6-11 *(Please Read)*
Forgiveness, just like love is a DECISION not a FEELING.
¹² And forgive us our debts, as we forgive our debtors.

PEOPLE WHO DO NOT KNOW HOW TO RECEIVE FORGIVENESS CAN'T GIVE FORGIVENESS because they don't really believe that they are forgiven.

God has offered you forgiveness and salvation at the cost of His Son's pain and life.

John 3:16 *(Please Read)*

As strange and illogical as it seems, may you receive grace to receive forgiveness in Jesus name.

_____
_____
_____
_____
_____

Day 19

Matthew 6:12. Romans 5:6-11 *(Please Read)*
Forgiveness, just like love is a DECISION not a FEELING.
¹² And forgive us our debts, as we forgive our debtors.

UNFORGIVENESS ENSLAVES and TIES YOU TO YOUR PAST. It also STEALS THE JOY OF THE PRESENT.
Let me remind you again that you have your eyes in front of you because new things are happening in front of you not behind you.
Isaiah 43:19 *(Please Read)*
God has new things coming beloved.
This day may you receive an unavoidable grace to receive the new in Jesus name.

_____

_____

_____

_____

Day 20

Matthew 6:12. Romans 5:6-11 *(Please Read)*
Forgiveness, just like love is a DECISION not a FEELING.
¹² And forgive us our debts, as we forgive our debtors.

Never allow anyone or yourself to subtly bring you to a point where PAIN, BITTERNESS AND RECOUNTING OF SAD STORIES becomes your source of fuel, energy, motivation or personality.
The devil would have lured you into a temporary hell.
Don't let it happen PLEASE!
1John 2:9 *(Please Read)*
May the sacrifice of Jesus be your refuge forever, in Jesus name.

_____

_____

_____

_____

_____

Day 21

Matthew 6:12. Romans 5:6-11 *(Please Read)*
Forgiveness, just like love is a DECISION not a FEELING.

¹² And forgive us our debts, as we forgive our debtors.

EMPATHY and SYMPATHY IS NOT A CURE.

Although wonderful and highly recommendable, do not mistake the temporary feeling that comes from empathy and sympathy with the real cure that God alone offers through the efficacious blood of Jesus Christ.

Hebrews 9:14 *(Please Read)*
Your TRUE CURE AND HEALING is available TODAY, in Jesus name.

_____
_____
_____
_____
_____

Day 22

Matthew 6:12. Romans 5:6-11 (Please Read)
Forgiveness, just like love is a DECISION not a FEELING.
¹² And forgive us our debts, as we forgive our debtors.
SILENCE IS PERMISSION for your problems to remain the same. Communication is the oil that lubricates life, anyone that ignores it cannot have a fulfilled life. Take time to discuss issues which disturbs you with God.
It's childish to think that ignoring or closing your eyes makes a problem go away.
Colossians 4:6 (Please Read)
May God grant you wisdom of communication in Jesus name.

_____

_____

_____

_____

_____

Day 23

Matthew 6:12. Romans 5:6-11 *(Please Read)*
Forgiveness, just like love is a DECISION not a FEELING.

¹² And forgive us our debts, as we forgive our debtors.

Therefore choose to forgive today and THEN feel the effectual result of peace and calm that comes with it.

This day may you receive an unavoidable strength to overcome all bitterness and hurt in Jesus name.

_____

_____

_____

_____

_____

Day 24

Matthew 6:12. Romans 5:6-11 *(Please Read)*
Forgiveness, just like love is a DECISION not a FEELING.
¹² And forgive us our debts, as we forgive our debtors.
This reminder is necessary. Don't expect the person that hurt you to heal and restore you. They don't have such power and it will be too much for you to have such expectation. Healing and restoration belongs to God and God alone.
Psalms 147:13 *(Please Read)*
Therefore choose to forgive all hurt and breathe in fresher air. Today may your hurt and pain go away permanently so you shall be set free to raise your hand in worship in Jesus name.

_____

_____

_____

_____

_____

Day 25

Matthew 6:12. Romans 5:6-11 (Please Read)
Forgiveness, just like love is a DECISION not a FEELING.

¹² **And forgive us our debts, as we forgive our debtors.**

What you HATE and don't FORGIVE, you BECOME.

What you FORGIVE, you RELEASE yourself from BECOMING.

LUKE 6:35 (Please Read)

Therefore choose to forgive all hurt and rest in God's perfect presence today in Jesus name.

_____

_____

_____

_____

Day 26

Matthew 18:21-22 *(Please Read)*
Forgiveness, just like love is a DECISION not a FEELING.
¹² And forgive us our debts, as we forgive our debtors.

When the Lord says we should forgive seventy times seven times, He is actually suggesting constant forgiveness.

Every conflict and disagreement requires two people. Thus, equal responsibility is on both individuals to forgive.

MAKE A DECISION TO FORGIVE EACH AND EVERY DAY.

_____

_____

_____

_____

_____

Day 27

Psalm 130:4 *(Please Read)*
Forgiveness, just like love is a DECISION not a FEELING.
¹² And forgive us our debts, as we forgive our debtors.

King David tells us that faith and salvation are in God.
Man should totally trust His Words.
There is no impeccable man. So, have faith and hope.

Your HEALING is accessible TODAY, in Jesus name.

_____

_____

_____

_____

Day 28

Matthew 26:28 *(Please Read)*
Forgiveness, just like love is a DECISION not a FEELING.
¹² And forgive us our debts, as we forgive our debtors.

God died for all of us, so our sins would be forgiven. If He could give himself for FORGIVENESS to the entire world, we could also forgive our fellowman. Through forgiveness we are closer to our Lord.

_____

_____

_____

_____

_____

Day 29

Mark 1:4 *(Please Read)*
Forgiveness, just like love is a DECISION not a FEELING.
¹² And forgive us our debts, as we forgive our debtors.

John the Baptist preached before Jesus Christ. He was the one who paved Christ's road. In the desert he preached about baptism for absolution of all sins. So shall we, taught with this call, to be baptized in the Truth of Christ and that baptism of the heart, mind and body should be our road toward FORGIVENESS and ETERNAL LIFE.

_____

_____

_____

_____

_____

Day 30

Luke 1:77 *(Please Read)*
Forgiveness, just like love is a DECISION not a FEELING.
¹² And forgive us our debts, as we forgive our debtors.

Jesus Christ the salvation of the world.
God came down on earth became a man and died so others would be forgiven.

Forgiveness is the Lord's will among men.
He has forgiven sins of people so WE should also forgive sins of others by this we will all be welcomed in the Lord's arms.

_____

_____

_____

_____

_____

Day 31

God's grace has blessed you with 31 days of study on forgiveness.
QUESTION: "What are you going to do with the information"?
Keep in mind the following;

THE FIRST TO APOLOGIZE IS THE BRAVEST

THE FIRST TO FORGIVE IS THE STRONGEST

THE FIRST TO FORGET IS THE HAPPIEST

Romans 12:18 (Please Read)

God Himself shall openly reward you for your works this time in Jesus name.

_____

_____

_____

_____

_____

Further Reading & Meditation

Romans 5:6-11 (NKJV)

⁶ For when we were still without strength, in due time Christ died for the ungodly. ⁷ For scarcely for a righteous man will one die; yet perhaps for a good man someone would even dare to die. ⁸ But God demonstrates His own love toward us, in that while we were still sinners, Christ died for us. ⁹ Much more then, having now been justified by His blood, we shall be saved from wrath through Him. ¹⁰ For if when we were enemies we were reconciled to God through the death of His Son, much more, having been reconciled, we shall be saved by His life. ¹¹ And not only that, but we also rejoice in God through our Lord Jesus Christ, through whom we have now received the reconciliation.

Jesus Christ, with His coming to Earth, His life, death and resurrection, showed that forgiveness of sins is the Lord's decision aimed at all nations. Taught with Jesus Christ's example, we should forgive all always.

Forgive Past Hurts

Forgiveness does not mean pretending everything is "OK." It doesn't mean forgetting the hurt either.

Forgiveness is the act of surrendering our desire for revenge i.e. our desire to hurt someone for having hurt us. Not placing focus or energy on the PAST HURT, but rather moving forward from the PAST HURT.

Forgiveness is the gift we give ourselves that enables us to stop picking at the scab and start making a plan for healing.

Un-forgiveness is a strategy of the devil to keep you bound.

Do you notice that whenever you are not forgiving a hurt, you don't have a lasting happy moment?

Yes you were hurt badly, yes you were broken and mistreated in your former relationship(s). In fact you were probably abused while growing up, but that is not the end of the road. You still have greater things to achieve.

It is not worth it to allow yesterday ruin your today and keep you away from a brighter tomorrow.

Un-forgiveness ties you to an unchangeable past which hinders you from entering into your own unique future.

When you forgive, the darkness in your heart will give room for light of God's love.

The love of God will overwhelm and encapsulate you, giving you a brand new reason for moving forward. There wouldn't be any incidence of being unruly or unfriendly because the joy of the Holy Spirit has taken you over.

It is absolutely easy to forgive and forget hurts and live off pains and agony of a terrible past because of the forgiveness you have also received from Christ. Forgiveness is the only way to deal with hurt, disappointment and bitterness.

FORGIVE ALL PAST HURTS

"Past emotional, mental or physical abuse, or being deeply hurt or mistreated by a friend or an enemy, are common causes of depression.

You might have had your share of such experiences, bitterness, anger and unforgiveness are typical responses to such injustices suffered, but as these reactions hinder our walk with Christ, the Bible gives us ample instructions on how to overcome them.

In many of the mentioned cases, especially where abuse is involved, getting help from a trained Christian counsellor or a professional health care worker is very highly recommended if not absolutely necessary.

DON'T DWELL ON THE PAST.

_____

_____

_____

_____

_____

MEDITATION SCRIPTURES:

Luke 6:27-29 (NKJV)

²⁷ "But I say to you who hear: Love your enemies, do good to those who hate you, ²⁸ bless those who curse you, and pray for those who spitefully use you. ²⁹ To him who strikes you on the one cheek, offer the other also. And from him who takes away your cloak, do not withhold your tunic either.

Romans 12:14 (NKJV)

¹⁴ Bless those who persecute you; bless and do not curse.

ACTION POINT:

Now make a list on the next few pages on the notes lines provided, of all those people that you can think of that have hurt you or that you need to forgive, you can specify what they did and why and how you are going to forgive them, also write down what you need God to forgive you of, this helps to release and move on.

Say dear Lord, I release and forgive that person that has hurt me from the firm grip of my heart.

I allow your light to illuminate my heart and theirs. And I bless them as your Word says in Jesus name.

Notes:

Notes:

Notes:

Acts 10:43 *(Please Read)*

Forgiveness is not just an emotion but also a decision based on the freewill of every individual?

It is because every person, every Christian with his own will accepts whether to repent and to forgive? To forgive injustices and bad things done to him, He forgives consciously as the Lord Jesus Christ has done more than 2000 years.

With forgiveness, you become one of those who are ready to accept Jesus Christ as Lord and Savior. FORGIVENESS IS A PERSONAL DECISION.

_____

_____

_____

_____

_____

Acts 13:38 *(Please Read)*

WITHOUT FORGIVENESS THERE IS NO SALVATION. Jesus Christ, with His coming to Earth, took all sins, died and resurrected.

He enabled all people to be saved. If man accepts the Word of Christ written in Holy Bible, he willingly accepts to be called Christian.

_____

_____

_____

_____

_____

Acts 26:18 *(Please Read)*

[18] to open their eyes, in order to turn them from darkness to light, and from the power of Satan to God, that they may receive forgiveness of sins and an inheritance among those who are sanctified by faith in Me.'

_____

_____

_____

_____

2 Corinthians 2:5 *(Please Read)*

Man can be weak, he was created like that. With only one prick of a needle, we bleed. But man's weakness is not a flaw; it is given by creation. Man is often angry, sad, offended. Even in those moments, everyone deserves forgiveness.

_____

_____

_____

_____

_____

Ephesians 1:7 *(Please Read)*

To forgive someone is not an easy task. Insults could be hard, deep, especially if coming from people close to us. In those situations, we are offended, with boiled emotions. But in moments like that we should forget our emotions and do the right thing. As the Lord Jesus Christ willingly gave His blood for us, we also have to CONSCIOUSLY FORGIVE and to show that our salvation was not in vain and that His blood and suffering were not worthless.

_____

_____

_____

_____

_____

Colossians 1:14 *(Please Read)*

Christianity constantly calls for love and respect among Christians.
Only through love is possible to live together, in peace and harmony.

It is the same with love that Jesus Christ had toward human kind.
WITH LOVE COMES FORGIVENESS, there is no love without forgiveness.
Only by being filled with love we can forgive unconditionally.

_____

_____

_____

_____

_____

Hebrews 9:22 *(Please Read)*

Since in Christianity forgiveness is not just a feeling but a personal decision of each individual, forgiving can be hard. But that should not deceive or interfere with our ultimate decision to forgive. Jesus Christ gave His blood for our salvation, He gave the biggest sacrifice possible, He gave Himself. GREAT SUCCESS is from GREAT SACRIFICE.

_____

_____

_____

_____

_____

1 John 1:9 *(Please Read)*

9 *If we confess our sins, He is faithful and just to forgive us our sins and to cleanse us from all unrighteousness.*

All people are sinful; there are no doubts about that.

We can see from our everyday actions that we sin all the time, often unconsciously, but also consciously. But the Lord, with His coming to Earth and with His sufferings, showed us that He loves us and forgives us.

As the Lord forgives, we must forgive each other. TO NOT FORGIVE IS A SIN.

_____

_____

_____

_____

_____

Genesis 50:17 *(Please Read)*

'Thus you shall say to Joseph: "I beg you, please forgive the trespass of your brothers and their sin; for they did evil to you."' Now, please, forgive the trespass of the servants of the God of your father." And Joseph wept when they spoke to him.

Forgiveness is not just reserved for the Lord who unconditionally forgives us all because of His great love, but it is for people also IN JESUS' NAME. The Lord tells us to forgive all, not just loved ones. We have to forgive, not only to our father or mother, siblings or family members but to all. FORGIVE EVERYONE.
It is the Lord's command to all Christians, to follow His example.

Exodus 10:17 *(Please Read)*

*When you pray for forgiveness of your sins, do not pray only for yourself.
Pray for family members, for friends, for acquaintances, for those who are not your friends, for those who offended you or for those who hurt you.*

THE LORD IS GREAT AND FORGIVES EVERYONE.

Pray for forgiveness of everyone's sins since we are ALL God's children.

_____

_____

_____

_____

_____

When we talk about forgiveness, we have to remember that we aren't the only ones who have to forgive.

*We are also those who have to be forgiven.
Not just by our fellowmen but also by the Lord.*

PRAY FOR FORGIVENESS.

Leviticus 4:31 *(Please Read)*

How to sacrifice oneself for forgiveness?
Jesus Christ sacrificed himself, truly and honestly, for the sake of all of us. That is the biggest truth in Christianity, truth we all have to remember.
Every man, following Christ's example has to sacrifice something for the sake of FORGIVENESS.

To RENOUNCE some HABITS for SALVATION is NOT THAT MUCH TO ASK.

_____

_____

_____

_____

_____

2 Chronicles 6:21 *(Please Read)*

²¹ And may You hear the supplications of Your servant and of Your people Israel, when they pray toward this place. Hear from heaven Your dwelling place, and when You hear, forgive

Forgiveness is closely connected with honest prayer. Repentance is a very serious process in which man goes through different phases. We must DISMISS THE SIN COMPLETELY and constantly pray for forgiveness.

_____

_____

_____

_____

_____

2 Chronicles 6:30 (Please Read)

Man's heart is the center of all feelings.
It loves, hates, fears, prays.
Forgiveness is above all a personal decision.

Forgiveness starts in our mind but is accepted in our heart.
FOR GENUINE FORGIVENESS BOTH HEART AND MIND ARE NECESSARY.

_____

_____

_____

_____

_____

Psalm 19:12 *(Please Read)*

Man must always ask for forgiveness for his sins from the Lord.
He must be persistent. And must sometimes suffer and wait.

Since man is susceptible to sin that's why he HAS TO ASK FOR FORGIVENESS.
You certainly offended someone sometimes, without even knowing that.

PRAY FOR FORGIVENESS OF UNINTENTIONAL SINS.
God knows about them even if you don't.

_____

_____

_____

_____

_____

Psalm 32:1 *(Please Read)*

Blessed is he whose transgression is forgiven, Whose sin is covered.

David teaches us that BLESSED is the one whose sins God has forgiven. Indeed, it is the greatest thing that man can experience.

It is the purpose of a Christian to ACHIEVE ETERNAL LIFE.

Forgiveness leads towards eternal life.

_____

_____

_____

_____

_____

Matthew 6:14 *(Please Read)*

*Matthew tells us about the complexity of forgiveness in his Gospel.
He teaches us that the Lord will not forgive us if we do not forgive others.*

_____

_____

_____

_____

_____

Matthew 6:15 *(Please Read)*

*If we do not want to forgive others then God will not forgive us.
By rejection of forgiveness, man shows that he is proud, self righteous and heartless.*

SELFISHNESS DOESN'T GO WITH FORGIVENESS.

_____

_____

_____

_____

Matthew 9:1 - 2 *(Please Read)*

1. So He got into a boat, crossed over, and came to His own city. 2. Then behold, they brought to Him a paralytic lying on a bed. When Jesus saw their faith, He said to the paralytic, "Son, be of good cheer; your sins are forgiven you."

Forgiveness cannot be separated from faith. A true Christian must truly believe in God.

Matthew 9:5 *(Please Read)*

Jesus Christ forgave sins while He walked amongst us; this often made other people suspicious. Many were thinking that He was blasphemous, but those were the ones who did not recognized Jesus Christ as the Son of God and that He had power to forgive.

JESUS CHRIST WITH HIS POWER CAN FORGIVE SINS.

_____

_____

_____

_____

_____

Mark 4:12 *(Please Read)*

God's physical absence from our world doesn't mean He doesn't exist.
But man's idea being very pragmatic does not believe in something or someone until he sees it with his own eyes and hears it with his own ears. There were times when Jesus walked among people and healed the sick, but people refused to believe it. Just because of their rationality MANY MISSED OUT ON FORGIVENESS. You have to see Christ with your open heart.

_____

_____

_____

_____

_____

Mark 11:25 *(Please Read)*

[25] *"And whenever you stand praying, if you have anything against anyone, forgive him, that your Father in heaven may also forgive you your trespasses.*

Forgiveness is part of the prayer group.

IF YOU HAVE ANY ISSUE WITH ANYONE FORGIVE.

_____

_____

_____

_____

_____

Luke 5:23 *(Please Read)*

²³ *Which is easier, to say, 'Your sins are forgiven you,' or to say, 'Rise up and walk'?* Every man has a dilemma, is it easier to just say we forgive or to show it by action that we have truly forgiven to our neighbor?
In Christianity it is known that faith without actions is weak. So, when you forgive, where possible show it to your neighbor.
LET THEM KNOW.

_____

_____

_____

_____

_____

Luke 6:37 *(Please Read)*

As we know, forgiveness is very important in Christian tradition and in the life of every Christian. But with forgiveness comes a powerful virtue – to be nonjudgmental. So, besides your praying for forgiveness, don't be judgmental to others.
Everyone often makes mistakes.
Don't be proud.

Luke 7:43 *(Please Read)*

⁴³ Simon answered and said, "I suppose the one whom he forgave more." And He said to him, "You have rightly judged."

Luke 7:47 *(Please Read)*

*Through your forgiveness show your love.
Always find love for people.*

*Your every action has to be filled with love and care.
FORGIVENESS SHOULDN'T BE A FORMALITY.
It has to be honest and enthusiastic so those who
you forgive will feel your love and devotion.*

_____

_____

_____

_____

_____

Luke 12:10 *(Please Read)*

God assures us THAT THOSE WHO TRULY REPENT WILL BE FORGIVEN.

_____

_____

_____

_____

Luke 17:3 *(Please Read)*

Even if someone does something wrong to us, it doesn't mean we should not react.
However our reaction of discontent shouldn't become aggression. We can let the person know that they did something wrong and painful BUT ALWAYS HAVE A PLACE FOR FORGIVENESS IN YOUR HEART.
Forgive every time, no matter what the sin is.

_____

_____

_____

_____

_____

Luke 17:4 *(Please Read)*

Don't pay attention on how many times someone did something bad and sinful or animosity toward you. If they did it ten times, forgive them.

However this does not mean that you put yourself in a position to be intentionally abused or violated the Bible teaches us to guard our heart.

John 20:23 *(Please Read)*

Forgive everyone that asks you, just as our Lord, Jesus Christ did. Whether their repentance is truthful or not, you forgive anyway. Sin is like a knot, if forgiveness does not untangle it, it remains. FORGIVENESS DESTROYS SINS.

_____

_____

_____

_____

_____

Acts 8:22 *(Please Read)*

Many sins and mistakes man does in his mind and thinks is not dangerous since no one knows about it and no action was taken.
THERE ARE NO SECRETS IN FRONT OF GOD.
Pray for forgiveness of those sins, too.

_____

_____

_____

_____

Romans 4:7 *(Please Read)*

Apostle Paul teaches Christians in Rome that it is best for Christians to forget about their lawlessness and to repent for all wrongs done to God and to people. He who sincerely asks God for forgiveness will receive His forgiveness.

_____

_____

_____

_____

_____

2 Corinthians 2:10 *(Please Read)*

¹⁰ Now whom you forgive anything, I also forgive. For if indeed I have forgiven anything, I have forgiven that one[a] for your sakes in the presence of Christ,

2 Corinthians 12:13 (Please Read)

*Do not be afraid to point out others sins.
Do not judge, but be ready and open to others when they point out your mistakes.
Help each other in order to come closer to God.*

_____

_____

_____

_____

_____

Colossians 3:13 *(Please Read)*

Forgiveness is compassion. This action is twofold. You always forgive someone and someone always forgives you. It is the way the Lord teaches us. As Christianity is a about compassion, so is forgiveness. FORGIVE EACH OTHER.
THIS IS GOD'S STANDARD.

_____

_____

_____

_____

_____

Hebrews 8:12 *(Please Read)*

As God forgives and forgets, you also forgive and move forward.

If you forgive someone's injustice, do not mention it again.
WHEN YOU FORGIVE, FORGET ABOUT IT.

_____

_____

_____

_____

_____

Hebrews 10:18 *(Please Read)*

If your sin is forgiven once, intend to never do it again.

_____

_____

_____

_____

_____

James 5:15 *(Please Read)*

Great power lies in true prayer for forgiveness. If a man forgives with an honest heart, it means a lot in the eyes of our Lord.

The strength of our forgiveness is strong IT CAN HEAL SICK PEOPLE.

***1 John 2:12** (Please Read)*

I write to you, little children, Because your sins are forgiven you for His name's sake.

_____

_____

_____

_____

_____

Job 9:15 *(Please Read)*

Forgiveness is not just some rational thing between two or more individuals or between man and God. Forgiveness is much more.
We have to pray for mercy as Job did. God assures us that our prayer wouldn't be for nothing.

_____

_____

_____

_____

Job 41:3 *(Please Read)*

Forgiveness is not just something where interested parties fulfilled their obligations. No, FORGIVENESS is the POWER of GOD that is given to man and doesn't allow him to remain in a fallen state, but encourages him to constantly try harder. God forgives man even though man constantly makes mistakes.

_____

_____

_____

_____

_____

Romans 9:16 *(Please Read)*

The power of forgiveness is strong. If something is bound on Earth, then it is also bound in Heaven. And if something is unbound on Earth, it will be unbounded in Heaven also. But the power of forgiveness comes from the power and mercy of God. FORGIVENESS IS THE AMAZING MERCY OF GOD.

_____

_____

_____

_____

_____

Leviticus 4:26 *(Please Read)*

Forgiveness, as a process, should not be a partial thing or an event.

When man regrets and repents, he is doing it for everything he has done. Every Christian wants to be without sins when the Judgment Day comes.

_____

_____

_____

_____

_____

Leviticus 5:10 *(Please Read)*

Do not be surprised if sometimes your sacrifice becomes an example for others to learn from, if God chooses you to be an example to others. Don't be quick to get angry be gentle and calm. If you accept your sacrifice without complain, the Lord will forgive you and make it work together for your good.

SACRIFICE IS IN THE PERSEVERANCE.

_____

_____

_____

_____

Leviticus 5:13 *(Please Read)*

The essential part of life of every Christian is confession.
Confession is man's way to talk to God, with or without an intermediary.
In each case, through confession, God forgives sins.

The Priest/Pastor is the one who in the name of God reassures us of forgiveness of our sins.

_____

_____

_____

_____

Leviticus 5:16 *(Please Read)*

True believers and Christians are not afraid of confession.
A credible and experienced Pastor or Minister is a good guide to lead people through the process of confession and can encourage and empower them with the strength to ask the Lord for forgiveness. Who is honest in front of a Pastor or Minister of God is honest in front of God Almighty also.

Leviticus 6:7 *(Please Read)*

The Priest/Pastor can assist to liberate you with prayer and sound Biblical advice. Liberation does not justify what happened, it doesn't mean it was alright or that a person that has hurt you is now automatically welcomed back into your life. FORGIVENESS MAKES YOU AT PEACE WITHIN YOURSELF TO COPE WITH WHAT HAS HAPPENED.

It means you are ready to release that pain or negative thoughts in order to focus on something that fulfills you.

_____

_____

_____

_____

_____

Leviticus 19:22 *(Please Read)*

The Pastor/Priest is there to help take away your pain through confession. FORGIVENESS IS SOMETHING YOU COULD DO FOR OTHERS AND FOR YOURSELF.

You could choose to live your life based on pain and anger or you can accept everything that has happened and carry on.

It doesn't always mean that you will forget what someone has done, it means you will stop being bitter.

_____

_____

_____

_____

_____

Numbers 14:19 *(Please Read)*

God has always forgiven people. Forgiveness is a characteristic of those who are strong and confident.

Find inside you the strength to deal with situations and overcome it since it is not a "crime" to forgive those who offended you.

It is a crime to be imprisoned in pain, anger and negative emotions that do not allow you to live your life to its full potential.

_____

_____

_____

_____

Numbers 15:25 (Please Read)

There were times when people offered animals as a sacrifice.
Then Christ gave himself as the sacrifice for people's sins.
It was the biggest sacrifice of all.
OFFER A SACRIFICE when you ask for forgivenes.
A sacrifice could be giving God praise and worship in singing, making a new commitment to serve God, sharing your testimony, helping others, financial, supporting your Pastor the best way possible.

_____

_____

_____

_____

_____

1 Samuel 15:25 *(Please Read)*

Forgiveness of the sins is deeply connected with God.
He who forgives and he who is forgiven are united in God and have the same goal.
IN THE MOMENT OF FORGIVENESS, GOD IS WITH THEM God's connection between people is huge and because of that, the need for forgiveness is also huge.

_____

_____

_____

_____

_____

Forgiveness is the biggest and most beautiful expression of love. One must not be vengeful and selfish since those things that happened, could not be undone, you will only suffer if you live your life like that.

Forgive move on and you're in love with your life.

FORGIVENESS IS LOVE.

_____

_____

_____

_____

_____

1 Kings 8:30 *(Please Read)*

Man must pray honestly and truthfully for forgiveness.

Prayer must show man's honesty and his intention to change his way of living. If sin was the way of someone's life, truthfulness of his change is shown in changing his life of sin.

PRAYER FOR FORGIVENESS MUST BE FOLLOWED WITH ACTIONS.

_____

_____

_____

_____

A man that honestly asks for forgiveness receives a sign from God.
He is shown a sign that points toward the right direction.
Pray to the Lord to give you the sign that shows you are on the right path. FORGIVENESS HAS THE RIGHT PATH.

The right path is revealed by God and you have to follow it.
GOD IS A MERCIFUL AND GRACIOUS GOD.

_____

_____

_____

_____

_____

Whatever person thinks, they could lie to God.
And falsely repent cannot pose himself as a true and honest Christian.

He could maybe fool others, but he cannot fool God.
God has created man and knows his heart.
So when you pray for forgiveness PRAYER MUST BE SINCERE AND GENUINE.

_____

_____

_____

_____

_____

*Insincerity does not lead toward forgiveness.
It only puts us further away from God and people.
It is not a virtue.*

INSINCERE REPENTANCE SADDENS GOD.

Psalm 103:1-3 (NKJV)

PRAISE FOR THE LORD'S MERCIES

Bless the Lord, O my soul;

And all that is within me, bless His holy name!

² Bless the Lord, O my soul,

And forget not all His benefits:

³ Who forgives all your iniquities,

Who heals all your diseases,

Let us always be grateful to God for blessing us, especially with the gift of FORGIVENESS which FORGIVES ALL OUR SINS. To God be the Glory and praise.

Notes:

Notes:

Notes:

Notes:

Notes:

Notes:

Notes:

Notes:

Notes:

Notes:

Notes:

Notes:

Notes:

Notes:

Notes:

Notes:

Notes:

Notes:

Notes:

Notes:

Notes:

Notes:

Notes:

Notes:

Notes:

Notes:

Notes:

Notes:

Notes:

Notes:

Notes:

Notes:

Notes:

Notes:

Notes:

For more titles from this author see

Dr Okwudili James Ezeh

www.lovingpoland.com

Imago Dei Ministries

Published by

Agape Behaviour Publishing

www.agapebehaviourpublishing.com

info@agapebehaviourpublishing.com

www.ingramcontent.com/pod-product-compliance
Lightning Source LLC
Chambersburg PA
CBHW030910080526
44589CB00010B/230